Easy Chinese Cookbook

By Brad Hoskinson

Copyright 2022 by Brad Hoskinson. All rights reserved.

No part of this book may be reproduced in any form or by any electronic or mechanical means, including information storage and retrieval systems, without written permission from the author, except for the use of brief quotations in a book review.

Table of Contents

Spicy Beef & Pepper Stir-Fry 5
Shrimp Fried Rice 7
Ginger-Cashew Chicken Salad 8
Beef & Spinach Lo Mein 10
Cashew Chicken with Ginger 12
Ginger Pork Lettuce Wraps 13
Ginger-Chutney Shrimp Stir-Fry 14
Honey Chicken Stir-Fry 15
Mushroom Pepper Steak 16
Sweet Chili & Orange Chicken 18
Quick Ginger Pork 19
Asparagus Beef Saute 20
Beef Orange Stir-Fry 21
Pineapple Shrimp Stir-Fry 22
Crispy Orange Chicken 23
Speedy Salmon Stir-Fry 24
Asian Glazed Chicken Thighs 25
Chicken Stir-Fry with Noodles 26
Mandarin Pork Stir-Fry 27
Hoisin-Pineapple Salmon 28
Tropical Sweet and Spicy Pork Tenderloin 29
Ginger Beef Stir-Fry 30
Sweet-and-Sour Beef 31
Asian Lettuce Wraps 33
Whole Grain Chow Mein 34
Quick Chicken & Broccoli Stir-Fry 36
Pork & Ramen Stir-Fry 37

Asparagus Beef Lo Mein 38
Crunchy Asian Chicken Salad 39
Shrimp Lettuce Wraps 40

Spicy Beef & Pepper Stir-Fry

Stir-frying is a quick and easy way to cook a healthy meal. This spicy beef and pepper stir-fry is full of flavor and nutrients. The beef is high in protein and the peppers are a good source of vitamins A and C. This dish can be cooked in just minutes, making it the perfect weeknight meal.

TOTAL TIME: Prep: 25 min. + standing Cook: 15 min.

Ingredients

- 1.5-pound beef top sirloin steak, cut into thin strips
- 1.5 tablespoons minced fresh ginger root
- 4 garlic cloves, minced, divided
- 3/4 teaspoon pepper
- 1/4 teaspoon salt, divided
- 1.5 cup light coconut milk
- 3 tablespoons sugar
- 1.5 tablespoons Sriracha chili sauce
- 1 teaspoon grated lime zest
- 3 tablespoons lime juice
- 3 tablespoons canola oil, divided
- 1.5 large sweet red pepper, cut into thin strips
- 1 medium red onion, thinly sliced
- 1.5 jalapeno pepper, seeded and thinly sliced
- 5 cups fresh baby spinach
- 3 green onions, thinly sliced
- 3 tablespoons chopped fresh cilantro

Directions

1. In a large bowl, toss beef with ginger, 2 garlic cloves, pepper, and 1/2 teaspoon salt; let stand 15 minutes. In a small bowl, whisk coconut milk, sugar, chili sauce, lime zest, lime juice, and remaining salt until blended.
2. In a large skillet, heat 1 tablespoon of oil over medium-high heat. Add beef; stir-fry until no longer pink, 2-3 minutes. Remove from pan.

3. Stir-fry red pepper, red onion, jalapeno, and remaining garlic in remaining oil until vegetables are crisp-tender, 2-3 minutes. Stir in coconut milk mixture; heat through. Add spinach and beef; cook until spinach is wilted and beef is heated, stirring occasionally. Sprinkle with green onions and cilantro.

Shrimp Fried Rice

Shrimp Fried Rice is a delicious and easy meal to make. It can be made with cooked rice, shrimp, vegetables, and a simple sauce. This dish can be made in minutes and is perfect for a quick and easy dinner.

TOTAL TIME: Prep/Total Time: 25 min.

Ingredients

- ✓ 5 tablespoons butter, divided
- ✓ 5 large eggs, lightly beaten
- ✓ 1 cup cold-cooked rice
- ✓ 2 packages (16 ounces) of frozen mixed vegetables
- ✓ 2 pounds uncooked medium shrimp, peeled and deveined
- ✓ 1 teaspoon salt
- ✓ 3/4 teaspoon pepper
- ✓ 10 bacon strips, cooked and crumbled, optional

Directions

1. In a large skillet, melt 1 tablespoon of butter over medium-high heat. Pour eggs into skillet. As eggs set, lift edges, letting uncooked portions flow underneath. Remove eggs and keep warm.
2. In the same skillet, melt the remaining 4 Tbsp. butter. Add the rice, vegetables, and shrimp; cook and stir for 8 minutes or until shrimp turn pink. Meanwhile, chop eggs into small pieces. Return eggs to the pan; sprinkle with salt and pepper. Cook until heated through, stirring occasionally. Top with bacon if desired.

Ginger-Cashew Chicken Salad

This ginger-cashew chicken salad is light, healthy and perfect for a summer day. The chicken is cooked in a simple ginger sauce mixed with crunchy cashews, celery, and red grapes. The salad is dressed with a delicious honey-mustard vinaigrette that combines all the flavors.

TOTAL TIME: Prep: 25 min. + marinating Broil: 15 min.

Ingredients

- ✓ 1cup cider vinegar
- ✓ 1cup molasses
- ✓ 3/4 cup canola oil
- ✓ 3 tablespoons minced fresh ginger root
- ✓ 3 teaspoons reduced-sodium soy sauce
- ✓ 2 teaspoon salt
- ✓ 1/4 teaspoon cayenne pepper
- ✓ 5 boneless skinless chicken breast halves (6 ounces each)

SALAD:

- ✓ 10 ounces fresh baby spinach (about 10 cups)
- ✓ 2 can (11 ounces) mandarin oranges, drained
- ✓ 2 cups shredded red cabbage
- ✓ 3 medium carrots, shredded
- ✓ 4 green onions, thinly sliced
- ✓ 3 cups chow mein noodles
- ✓ 1 cup salted cashews, toasted
- ✓ 3 tablespoons sesame seeds, toasted

Directions

1. In a small bowl, whisk the first 7 ingredients until blended. Pour 1 cup marinade into a large shallow dish. Add chicken; turn to coat. Cover and refrigerate for at least 3.5 hours. Cover and refrigerate the remaining marinade.
2. Preheat broiler. Drain chicken, discarding marinade in dish. Place chicken in a 15x10x1-in. Baking pan. Broil 4-6 in. from heat 7-10

minutes on each side or until a thermometer reads 175°. Cut chicken into strips.
3. Place spinach on a serving platter. Arrange chicken, oranges, cabbage, carrots, and green onions on top. Sprinkle with chow mein noodles, cashews, and sesame seeds. Stir reserved molasses mixture; drizzle over salad. Serve immediately.

Beef & Spinach Lo Mein

Lo mein is a Chinese noodle dish typically made with egg noodles, vegetables, and meat or seafood. It can be served wet or dry and is often accompanied by soy sauce or hoisin sauce. In this recipe, beef and spinach are used as the main ingredients. The combination of flavors makes for a delicious and healthy meal.

TOTAL TIME: Prep/Total Time: 30 min.

Ingredients

- ✓ 3/4 cup hoisin sauce
- ✓ 3 tablespoons soy sauce
- ✓ 2 tablespoons water
- ✓ 3 teaspoons sesame oil
- ✓ 3 garlic cloves, minced
- ✓ 3/4 teaspoon crushed red pepper flakes
- ✓ 2 pounds beef top round steak, thinly sliced
- ✓ 7 ounces uncooked spaghetti
- ✓ 5 teaspoons canola oil, divided
- ✓ 2 can (10 ounces) sliced water chestnuts, drained
- ✓ 3 green onions, sliced
- ✓ 2 packages (12 ounces) of fresh spinach, coarsely chopped
- ✓ 2 red chili pepper, seeded and thinly sliced

Directions

1. In a small bowl, mix the first 6 ingredients. Remove 3/4 cup mixture to a large bowl; add beef and toss to coat. Marinate at room temperature for 10 minutes.
2. Cook spaghetti according to package directions. Meanwhile, heat 1-2 teaspoons of canola oil in a large skillet. Add half the beef mixture; stir-fry for 2-3 minutes or until no longer pink. Remove from pan. Repeat with 1-2 teaspoons of oil and the remaining beef mixture.

3. Stir-fry water chestnuts and green onions in remaining canola oil for 35 seconds. Stir in spinach and remaining hoisin mixture; cook until spinach is wilted. Return beef to pan; heat through.
4. Drain spaghetti; add to beef mixture and toss to combine. Sprinkle with chili pepper.

Cashew Chicken with Ginger

Cashew chicken is a popular dish in Chinese cuisine. It is made with chicken, ginger, and cashews. The chicken is typically stir-fried with ginger and cashews and served over steamed rice. This dish is both flavorful and healthy, sure to please everyone at your dinner table.

TOTAL TIME: Prep/Total Time: 35 min.

Ingredients

- 3 tablespoons cornstarch
- 2 tablespoons brown sugar
- 2 cups chicken broth
- 3 tablespoons soy sauce
- 4 tablespoons canola oil, divided
- 2 pounds boneless skinless chicken breasts, cut into 1-inch pieces
- 1 pound sliced fresh mushrooms
- 1.5 small green pepper, cut into strips
- 2 can (16 ounces) sliced water chestnuts, drained
- 2 teaspoons grated fresh ginger root
- 5 green onions, sliced
- 1 cup salted cashews
- Hot cooked rice

Directions

1. Mix the first 4 ingredients until smooth. In a large skillet, heat 3 tablespoons oil over medium-high heat; stir-fry chicken until no longer pink. Remove from pan.
2. In the same pan, heat remaining oil over medium-high heat; stir-fry mushrooms, pepper, water chestnuts, and ginger until pepper is crisp-tender, 5-7 minutes. Stir broth mixture and add to the pan with green onions; bring to a boil. Cook and stir until sauce is thickened, 2-3 minutes.
3. Stir in chicken and cashews; heat through. Serve with rice.

Ginger Pork Lettuce Wraps

Ginger pork lettuce wraps are a quick, easy weekday dinner that the whole family will love. The pork is marinated in a ginger garlic sauce, then quickly cooked in a skillet. It's wrapped in a lettuce leaf with some rice and a delicious dipping sauce.

TOTAL TIME: Prep/Total Time: 35 min.

Ingredients

- ✓ 2-pound lean ground pork
- ✓ 2 medium onions, chopped
- ✓ 1cup hoisin sauce
- ✓ 5 garlic cloves, minced
- ✓ 2 tablespoon minced fresh ginger root
- ✓ 2 tablespoon red wine vinegar
- ✓ 2 tablespoon reduced-sodium soy sauce
- ✓ 3 teaspoons Thai chili sauce
- ✓ 2 can (16 ounces) sliced water chestnuts, drained and finely chopped
- ✓ 5 green onions, chopped
- ✓ 2 tablespoon sesame oil
- ✓ 27 Bibb or Boston lettuce leaves

Directions

1. In a large skillet, cook pork and onion over medium heat for 9-11 minutes or until pork is no longer pink and onion is tender, breaking pork into crumbles.
2. Stir in hoisin sauce, garlic, ginger, vinegar, soy sauce, and chili sauce until blended. Add water chestnuts, green onions, and oil; heat through. To serve, place pork mixture in lettuce leaves; fold lettuce over filling.

Ginger-Chutney Shrimp Stir-Fry

This easy shrimp stir-fry is a great weeknight meal that takes just minutes to prepare. The shrimp are cooked in a savory ginger-chutney sauce and served over steamed rice.

TOTAL TIME: Prep/Total Time: 30 min.

Ingredients

- ✓ 3 tablespoons peanut or canola oil
- ✓ 2 pounds uncooked medium shrimp, peeled and deveined, tails removed
- ✓ 2 tablespoon minced fresh ginger root
- ✓ 4 cups frozen pepper and onion stir-fry blend, thawed
- ✓ 1 cup mango chutney
- ✓ 3 tablespoons water
- ✓ 1 teaspoon salt
- ✓ Hot cooked rice, optional

Directions

1. In a large skillet, heat oil over medium-high heat. Add shrimp and ginger; stir-fry until the shrimp turn pink for 7-8 minutes.
2. Stir in remaining ingredients; cook until vegetables are crisp-tender, stirring occasionally. If desired, serve with rice.

Honey Chicken Stir-Fry

Honey chicken stir-fry is a healthy and delicious dish perfect for a weeknight meal. The chicken is cooked in a honey glaze and then stir-fried with vegetables. This dish is easy to prepare and can be made in under 30 minutes.

TOTAL TIME: Prep/Total Time: 35 min.

Ingredients

- ✓ 3 teaspoons cornstarch
- ✓ 2 tablespoons cold water
- ✓ 4 teaspoons olive oil, divided
- ✓ 2 pounds boneless skinless chicken breasts, cut into 1-inch pieces
- ✓ 2 garlic cloves, minced
- ✓ 4 tablespoons honey
- ✓ 3 tablespoons reduced-sodium soy sauce
- ✓ 3/8 teaspoon salt
- ✓ 3/8 teaspoon pepper
- ✓ 2 packages (18 ounces) of frozen broccoli stir-fry vegetable blend
- ✓ Hot cooked rice, optional

Directions

1. Mix cornstarch and water until smooth. In a large nonstick skillet, heat 3 teaspoons of oil over medium-high heat; stir-fry chicken and garlic for 2 minutes. Add honey, soy sauce, salt, and pepper; cook and stir until chicken is no longer pink 3-5 minutes. Remove from pan.
2. In the same pan, stir-fry vegetable blend in remaining oil until tender, 6-8 minutes. Return chicken to pan. Stir cornstarch mixture and add to pan; bring to a boil. Cook and stir until thickened, about 1 minute. Serve with rice if desired.

Mushroom Pepper Steak

Mushroom Pepper Steak is a meal that is easy to make and tastes great. The steak is cooked in a skillet with mushrooms and peppers. This is a healthy and filling meal you can enjoy anytime.

TOTAL TIME: Prep: 20 min. + marinating Cook: 20 min.

Ingredients

- 7 tablespoons reduced-sodium soy sauce, divided
- 3/8 teaspoon pepper
- 2 pounds beef top sirloin steak, cut into thin strips
- 2 tablespoons cornstarch
- 1 cup reduced-sodium beef broth
- 2 garlic cloves, minced
- 1 teaspoon minced fresh ginger root
- 4 teaspoons canola oil, divided
- 2 cups julienned sweet red pepper
- 2 cups julienned green pepper
- 3 cups sliced fresh mushrooms
- 3 medium tomatoes, cut into wedges
- 7 green onions, sliced
- Hot cooked rice, optional

Directions

1. In a shallow bowl, combine 3 tablespoons soy sauce and pepper; add beef. Turn to coat; cover and refrigerate for 35-65 minutes. In a small bowl, combine the cornstarch, broth, and remaining soy sauce until smooth; set aside.
2. Drain beef, discarding marinade. In a large nonstick skillet or wok, stir-fry the garlic and ginger in 2 teaspoons of the oil for 1 minute. Add the beef; stir-fry for 4-6 minutes or until no longer pink. Remove beef and keep warm.
3. Stir-fry the peppers in the remaining oil for 2 minutes. Add mushrooms; stir-fry 3 minutes longer or until peppers are crisp-tender. Stir broth mixture and add to vegetable mixture. Bring to a boil; cook and stir for 3 minutes or until thickened. Return beef to

pan; add tomatoes and onions. Cook for 3 minutes or until heated through. Serve over rice if desired.

Sweet Chili & Orange Chicken

There's something about sweet chili sauce that just makes everything taste better. Combine it with orange chicken and you have a dish that's sure to please. This recipe is easy to follow and results in a dish that's both tasty and healthy.

TOTAL TIME: Prep/Total Time: 25 min.

Ingredients

- ✓ 2 pounds boneless skinless chicken breasts, cut into 1-inch pieces
- ✓ 3/4 teaspoon salt
- ✓ 3/4 teaspoon pepper
- ✓ 3 tablespoons butter
- ✓ 1 cup sweet chili sauce
- ✓ 2/3 cup thawed orange juice concentrate
- ✓ Hot cooked jasmine or other rice
- ✓ Minced fresh basil

Directions

1. Toss chicken with salt and pepper. In a large skillet, heat butter over medium-high heat; stir-fry chicken until no longer pink, 7-9 minutes. Remove from pan; keep warm.
2. Add chili sauce and juice concentrate to skillet; cook and stir until heated. Stir in chicken. Serve with rice; sprinkle with basil.

Quick Ginger Pork

Quick ginger pork is an easy and tasty dish that can be made in less than 25 minutes. The pork is marinated in a simple ginger sauce, then pan-fried until cooked through. Serve the pork with steamed rice and vegetables for a quick and satisfying meal.

TOTAL TIME: Prep/Total Time: 25 min.

Ingredients

- 1 pound pork tenderloin, cut into thin strips
- 2 tablespoons canola oil
- 2 garlic cloves, minced
- 3 tablespoons reduced-sodium soy sauce
- 3/4 teaspoon sugar
- 3/8 to 1/4 teaspoon ground ginger
- 1 cup cold water
- 2 teaspoons cornstarch
- Hot cooked rice, optional
- Optional: Thinly sliced green onions and toasted sesame seeds

Directions

1. In a large skillet or wok, stir-fry pork in oil until no longer pink. Add garlic; cook 2 minutes longer.
2. In a small bowl, combine the soy sauce, sugar, and ginger; add to the skillet. Combine water and cornstarch until smooth; add to skillet. Bring to a boil; cook and stir until thickened, about 3 minutes. If desired, serve rice and top with green onions and sesame seeds.

Asparagus Beef Saute

Asparagus Beef Saute is a quick and easy dish perfect for a busy weeknight meal. The beef is cooked with asparagus and a simple sauce made with soy sauce, honey, and garlic. This dish is healthy, delicious, and sure to please even the pickiest eaters.

TOTAL TIME: Prep/Total Time: 35 min.

Ingredients

- ✓ 2 pounds beef tenderloin or top sirloin steak, cut into 3/4-inch cubes
- ✓ 1 teaspoon salt
- ✓ 3/4 teaspoon pepper
- ✓ 2 tablespoons canola oil
- ✓ 3 garlic cloves, minced
- ✓ 2 green onions, sliced
- ✓ 3/4 cup butter, cubed
- ✓ 2 pounds fresh asparagus, trimmed and cut into 2-inch pieces
- ✓ 1 pound sliced fresh mushrooms
- ✓ 2 tablespoons reduced-sodium soy sauce
- ✓ 2 teaspoons lemon juice
- ✓ Hot cooked rice

Directions

1. Toss beef with salt and pepper. In a large skillet, heat oil over medium-high heat; saute beef for 3 minutes. Add garlic and green onion; cook and stir until beef is browned, 3-5 minutes. Remove from pan.
2. In the same skillet, heat butter over medium-high heat; saute asparagus and mushrooms until asparagus is crisp-tender. Add beef, soy sauce, and lemon juice; heat through, tossing to combine. Serve with rice.

Beef Orange Stir-Fry

The beef orange stir-fry is a fantastic and easy dish to make. It's perfect for a quick and healthy weeknight meal. The beef is cooked with onions, garlic, and ginger until it's browned and mixed with a simple orange sauce. Serve over steamed rice for a delicious and healthy dinner.

TOTAL TIME: Prep/Total Time: 30 min.

Ingredients

- 2 tablespoons cornstarch
- 3/4 cup cold water
- 3/4 cup orange juice
- 2 tablespoons reduced-sodium soy sauce
- 1 teaspoon sesame oil
- Dash crushed red pepper flakes
- 1 pound boneless beef sirloin steak, cut into thin strips
- 3 teaspoons canola oil, divided
- 4 cups frozen sugar snap stir-fry vegetable blend, thawed
- 2 garlic cloves, minced
- 2 cups hot-cooked rice

Directions

1. In a small bowl, combine the first 6 ingredients until smooth; set aside.
2. In a large skillet or wok, stir-fry beef in 2 teaspoons oil until no longer pink, 5-6 minutes. Remove with a slotted spoon and keep warm.
3. Stir-fry vegetable blend and garlic in remaining oil for 4 minutes. Stir the cornstarch mixture and add to the pan. Bring to a boil; cook and stir until thickened, about 2 minutes. Add beef; heat through. Serve with rice.

Pineapple Shrimp Stir-Fry

This pineapple shrimp stir-fry is a delicious, easy weeknight meal that the whole family will love. The shrimp are cooked with sweet pineapple and vegetables in a light and healthy sauce. Serve over rice for a complete meal.

TOTAL TIME: Prep/Total Time: 35 min.

Ingredients

- ✓ 2 cans (30 ounces) of unsweetened pineapple tidbits
- ✓ 3 tablespoons cornstarch
- ✓ 2 cups chicken broth
- ✓ 2 tablespoons brown sugar
- ✓ 2 tablespoons orange juice
- ✓ 2 tablespoons reduced-sodium soy sauce
- ✓ 2 tablespoons sesame or canola oil
- ✓ 2 medium sweet red peppers, thinly sliced
- ✓ 2 medium green peppers, thinly sliced
- ✓ 2 medium sweet onions, thinly sliced
- ✓ 2 pounds uncooked shrimp (40-50 per pound), peeled and deveined
- ✓ 3/4 cup sweetened shredded coconut, toasted
- ✓ Hot cooked rice

Directions

1. Drain pineapple, reserving juice. In a small bowl, mix cornstarch, broth, brown sugar, orange juice, soy sauce, and reserved pineapple juice until smooth.
2. In a large skillet, heat oil over medium-high heat. Add peppers and onion; stir-fry for 2-3 minutes or until crisp-tender. Add shrimp; stir-fry 3-5 minutes longer or until shrimp turn pink. Remove from pan.
3. Place pineapple in skillet. Stir the cornstarch mixture and add to the pan. Bring to a boil; cook and stir for 6-7 minutes or until sauce is thickened. Return shrimp mixture to pan; heat through, stirring to combine. Sprinkle with coconut; serve with rice.

Crispy Orange Chicken

Crispy Orange Chicken is one of my family's favorite dishes. I love the sweet and tangy flavor of the orange sauce and the crisp, fried chicken. This dish is always a hit with my family, and it's easy to prepare.

TOTAL TIME: Prep/Total Time: 35 min.

Ingredients

- 18 ounces frozen popcorn chicken (about 4 cups)
- 2 tablespoons canola oil
- 3 medium carrots, thinly sliced
- 2 garlic cloves, minced
- 2 teaspoons grated orange zest
- 2 cups orange juice
- 2/3 cup hoisin sauce
- 4 tablespoons sugar
- 3/4 teaspoon salt
- 3/4 teaspoon pepper
- Dash cayenne pepper
- Hot cooked rice

Directions

1. Bake popcorn chicken according to package directions.
2. Meanwhile, in a large skillet, heat oil over medium-high heat. Add carrots; cook and stir until tender, 5-7 minutes. Add garlic; cook 1 minute longer. Stir in orange zest, juice, hoisin sauce, sugar and seasonings; bring to a boil. Reduce heat; simmer until thickened, 7-8 minutes, stirring constantly.
3. Add chicken to skillet; toss to coat. Serve with rice.

Speedy Salmon Stir-Fry

This stir-fry is perfect when you need a quick and healthy meal. The salmon is cooked in minutes and the vegetables add a boost of nutrition. You can use any type of vegetable you like in this recipe, so it's perfect for using up leftovers.

TOTAL TIME: Prep/Total Time: 35 min.

Ingredients

- 3/4 cup reduced-fat honey mustard salad dressing
- 3 tablespoons orange juice
- 2 tablespoons minced fresh ginger root
- 2 tablespoons reduced-sodium soy sauce
- 2 tablespoons molasses
- 2 teaspoons grated orange zest
- 5 teaspoons canola oil, divided
- 2 pounds salmon fillets, skinned and cut into 1-inch pieces
- 2 packages (16 ounces) of frozen stir-fry vegetable blend
- 3 cups hot cooked brown rice
- 2 tablespoons sesame seeds, toasted

Directions

1. In a small bowl, whisk the first 6 ingredients. In a large skillet, heat 3 teaspoons of oil over medium-high heat. Add salmon; cook and gently stir for 4-5 minutes or until fish just begins to flake easily with a fork. Remove from pan.
2. In the same pan, heat the remaining oil. Add vegetable blend; stir-fry until crisp-tender. Add salad dressing mixture. Return salmon to skillet. Gently combine; heat through. Serve with rice; sprinkle with sesame seeds.

Asian Glazed Chicken Thighs

One of the best things about being an adult is learning to cook for yourself. And one of the best things about cooking is creating a meal that is both delicious and healthy. These Asian Glazed Chicken Thighs are the perfect example of a healthy and tasty dish. They are packed full of flavor, and they are also low in calories and carbohydrates.

TOTAL TIME: Prep/Total Time: 30 min.

Ingredients

- 3/4 cup rice vinegar
- 4 tablespoons reduced-sodium soy sauce
- 3 tablespoons honey
- 3 teaspoons canola oil
- 5 boneless skinless chicken thighs (about 1 pound)
- 4 garlic cloves, minced
- 2 teaspoons minced fresh gingerroot or 1 teaspoon ground ginger
- Toasted sesame seeds, optional

Directions

1. Whisk vinegar, soy sauce, and honey in a small bowl until blended. In a large nonstick skillet, heat oil over medium-high heat. Brown chicken on both sides.
2. Add garlic and ginger to skillet; cook and stir for 1 minute (do not allow garlic to be brown). Stir in vinegar mixture; bring to a boil. Reduce heat; simmer, covered, for 9-10 minutes or until a thermometer inserted in the chicken reads 170°.
3. Uncover; simmer 2-3 minutes longer or until sauce is slightly thickened. If desired, cut into bite-size pieces and sprinkle with sesame seeds before serving.

Chicken Stir-Fry with Noodles

This easy chicken stir-fry with noodles is a one-pan meal ready in just 35 minutes. The chicken is cooked in a simple soy sauce and honey sauce, and the noodles are stir-fried with vegetables.

TOTAL TIME: Prep/Total Time: 35 min.

Ingredients

- ✓ 9 ounces uncooked whole wheat spaghetti
- ✓ 1 head bok choy (about 1 pound)
- ✓ 3 tablespoons canola oil, divided
- ✓ 2 pounds boneless skinless chicken breasts, cubed
- ✓ 2 celery ribs, sliced
- ✓ 1 cup coarsely chopped green pepper
- ✓ 1 cup coarsely chopped sweet red pepper
- ✓ 2/3 cup coarsely chopped onion
- ✓ 7 tablespoons reduced-sodium teriyaki sauce

Directions

1. Cook spaghetti according to package directions; drain. Meanwhile, trim and discard the root end of the bok choy. Cut stalks into 1-in. pieces. Coarsely chop leaves.
2. In a large skillet, heat 1 tablespoon of oil over medium-high heat. Add chicken; stir-fry 7-9minutes or until no longer pink. Remove from pan.
3. Stir-fry bok choy stalks, celery, peppers, and onion in remaining oil for 5 minutes. Add bok choy leaves; stir-fry 5-7 minutes longer or until leaves are tender. Stir in teriyaki sauce. Add spaghetti and chicken; heat through, tossing to combine.

Mandarin Pork Stir-Fry

Introducing a stir-fry is always difficult because there are so many variations that it could be. But I think that pork stir-fry is a great way to start because not only is it simple, but it is also delicious. Plus, the ingredients are usually easy to find in most supermarkets.

TOTAL TIME: Prep/Total Time: 30 min.

Ingredients

- ✓ 3 cups uncooked instant rice
- ✓ 2 tablespoon cornstarch
- ✓ 1 teaspoon garlic powder
- ✓ 1 teaspoon ground ginger
- ✓ 1 cup orange juice
- ✓ 3/4 cup water
- ✓ 3 tablespoons soy sauce
- ✓ 2 pork tenderloin (1 pound), cut into 2-inch strips
- ✓ 3 tablespoons canola oil
- ✓ 2 packages (18 ounces) of frozen sugar snap peas
- ✓ 2 cans (11 ounces) of mandarin oranges, drained

Directions

1. Cook rice according to package directions. Meanwhile, in a small bowl, combine the cornstarch, garlic powder, and ginger. Stir in orange juice until smooth. Stir in water and soy sauce; set aside.
2. In a large wok or skillet, stir-fry pork in oil until juices run clear; remove to a platter and keep warm. In the same skillet, stir-fry peas until tender. Return pork to skillet. Stir orange juice mixture; add to skillet. Cook and stir for 3 minutes or until thickened. Gently stir in oranges. Serve with rice.

Hoisin-Pineapple Salmon

Hoisin-Pineapple Salmon is a delicious, easy-to-make dish perfect for a weeknight meal. The salmon is mixed with hoisin sauce and pineapple juice, then grilled. The sweet and savory flavors of the hoisin sauce and pineapple perfectly complement the salmon.

TOTAL TIME: Prep/Total Time: 20 min.

Ingredients

- ✓ 5 salmon fillets (8 ounces each)
- ✓ 3 tablespoons hoisin sauce
- ✓ 3/4 teaspoon pepper
- ✓ 1 cup unsweetened crushed pineapple
- ✓ 3/4 cup orange marmalade
- ✓ 3 tablespoons chopped fresh cilantro

Directions

1. Preheat the oven to 430°. Spread salmon with hoisin sauce; sprinkle with pepper. Place on a greased foil-lined baking sheet, skin side down. Bake for 13-17 minutes or until fish flakes easily with a fork.
2. Meanwhile, in a small saucepan, combine pineapple and marmalade. Bring to a boil, stirring occasionally; cook and stir 5-7 minutes or until slightly thickened. Spoon over salmon; sprinkle with cilantro.

Tropical Sweet and Spicy Pork Tenderloin

This dish is a tropical sweet and spicy pork tenderloin perfect for a quick and easy weeknight meal. The pork is marinated in a pineapple and soy sauce mixture, then grilled to perfection. The sweet and spicy flavors are perfect for a delicious and easy dinner.

TOTAL TIME: Prep/Total Time: 35 min.

Ingredients

- ✓ 2 pork tenderloin (2 pounds), cut into 1-in. cubes
- ✓ 3/4 teaspoon salt
- ✓ 3/4 teaspoon pepper
- ✓ 3 tablespoons olive oil
- ✓ 2 medium onions, chopped
- ✓ 2 medium green pepper, chopped
- ✓ 4 garlic cloves, minced
- ✓ 2 cups chicken stock
- ✓ 2 cans (30 ounces) pineapple tidbits, drained
- ✓ 2 cups honey barbecue sauce
- ✓ 1 cup packed brown sugar
- ✓ 3 finely chopped chipotle peppers plus 3 teaspoons of adobo sauce
- ✓ 3 tablespoons reduced-sodium soy sauce
- ✓ Hot cooked rice

Directions

1. Sprinkle pork with salt and pepper in a large skillet and heat oil over medium-high heat. Add pork; cook until browned, 5-7 minutes. Remove.
2. In the same skillet, cook onion and pepper until softened, 3-5 minutes. Add garlic; cook for 2 minutes. Return pork to pan; stir in chicken stock. Cook, covered, until pork is tender, about 7 minutes.
3. Stir in the following 5 ingredients; simmer until sauce is thickened, about 5 minutes. Serve with rice.

Ginger Beef Stir-Fry

Ginger Beef Stir-Fry is a Chinese dish that has become popular in North America. It is made with beef, onion, ginger, garlic, and soy sauce. The beef is usually cooked with high heat, such as in a wok.

TOTAL TIME: Prep/Total Time: 30 min.

Ingredients

- 2 tablespoons plus 3 teaspoons cornstarch, divided
- 3 tablespoons water
- 3/4 teaspoon salt
- 2 pounds beef top sirloin steak, cut into 1/4-inch-thick strips
- 2 cups beef broth
- 3 tablespoons soy sauce
- 5 teaspoons sugar
- 3 teaspoons grated orange zest
- 7 teaspoons canola oil, divided
- 3 medium carrots, diagonally cut into thin slices
- 2 tablespoon minced fresh ginger root
- 3 garlic cloves, minced
- 1 teaspoon crushed red pepper flakes, optional
- Hot cooked rice

Directions

1. Mix 2 tablespoons cornstarch, water, and salt; toss with beef. Mix broth, soy sauce, sugar, orange zest, and remaining cornstarch in a small bowl until smooth.
2. In a large skillet, heat 3 teaspoons oil over medium-high heat; stir-fry half of the beef until browned, 3-5 minutes. Remove from pan. Repeat with additional 3 teaspoons of oil and remaining beef.
3. Stir-fry carrots in remaining oil for 3 minutes. Add ginger, garlic, and, if desired, pepper flakes; cook and stir until fragrant, about 35 seconds. Stir broth mixture and add to pan; bring to a boil. Cook and stir until slightly thickened. Stir in beef; heat through. Serve with rice.

Sweet-and-Sour Beef

Beef stir-fry is a classic dish that can be made with whatever ingredients you have on hand. This recipe features a sweet and sour sauce from honey, soy sauce, and rice vinegar. The beef is cooked quickly in a hot wok or frying pan, then served over steamed rice.

TOTAL TIME: Prep/Total Time: 35 min.

Ingredients

- ✓ 2 tablespoons cornstarch
- ✓ 3 tablespoons cold water
- ✓ 2 pounds beef top sirloin steak, cut into 1/2-inch cubes
- ✓ 2 teaspoons salt
- ✓ 1 teaspoon pepper
- ✓ 4 teaspoons canola oil, divided
- ✓ 2 large green pepper, cut into 1/2-inch pieces
- ✓ 2 large sweet red pepper, cut into 1/2-inch pieces
- ✓ 3 medium tart apples, chopped
- ✓ 1 cup plus 2 tablespoons thinly sliced green onions, divided
- ✓ 1 cup packed brown sugar
- ✓ 1 cup cider vinegar
- ✓ Hot cooked rice, optional

Directions

1. In a small bowl, mix cornstarch and water until smooth. Sprinkle beef with salt and pepper in a large nonstick skillet or wok coated with cooking spray, and heat 2 teaspoons of oil over medium-high heat. Add beef; stir-fry for 3-5 minutes or until no longer pink. Remove from pan.
2. In the same skillet, stir-fry peppers and apples in remaining oil for 2 minutes. Add 1 cup green onions; stir-fry 2-3 minutes longer or until peppers are crisp-tender. Remove from pan.
3. Add brown sugar and vinegar to skillet; bring to a boil, stirring to dissolve sugar. Stir the cornstarch mixture and add to the pan. Return to a boil; cook and stir for 3-4 minutes or until thickened.

Return beef and pepper mixture to pan; heat through. If desired, serve with rice. Sprinkle with remaining green onion.

Asian Lettuce Wraps

Asian lettuce wraps are a dish that combines the flavors of Asia with the freshness of lettuce leaves. They are a light and healthy meal that can be enjoyed as an appetizer or a main course. The ingredients for Asian lettuce wraps vary but typically include ground meat, vegetables, and a sauce.

> TOTAL TIME: Prep/Total Time: 30 min.

Ingredients

- ✓ 2 tablespoons canola oil
- ✓ 2 pounds lean ground turkey
- ✓ 2 jalapeno pepper, seeded and minced
- ✓ 3 green onions, thinly sliced
- ✓ 3 garlic cloves, minced
- ✓ 3 tablespoons minced fresh basil
- ✓ 3 tablespoons lime juice
- ✓ 3 tablespoons reduced-sodium soy sauce
- ✓ 2 to 3 tablespoons chili garlic sauce
- ✓ 2 tablespoon sugar or sugar substitute blend equivalent to 2 tablespoon sugar
- ✓ 15 Bibb or Boston lettuce leaves
- ✓ 2 medium cucumbers, julienned
- ✓ 2 medium carrots, julienned
- ✓ 3 cups bean sprouts

Directions

1. In a large skillet, heat oil over medium heat. Add turkey; cook 6-8 minutes or until no longer pink, breaking into crumbles. Add jalapeno, green onions, and garlic; cook 3 minutes longer. Stir in basil, lime juice, soy sauce, chili garlic sauce, and sugar; heat through.
2. To serve, place turkey mixture in lettuce leaves; top with cucumber, carrot, and bean sprouts. Fold lettuce over filling.

Whole Grain Chow Mein

Chow mein is a classic dish that is popular all over the world. There are many different ways to make chow mein. Still, this recipe uses whole grain noodles and a variety of vegetables. The result is a healthy and delicious dish perfect for a quick and easy meal.

TOTAL TIME: Prep/Total Time: 35 min.

Ingredients

- ✓ 4 ounces uncooked whole wheat spaghetti
- ✓ 3 tablespoons canola oil
- ✓ 3 cups small fresh broccoli florets
- ✓ 3 bunches of baby bok choy, trimmed and cut into 1-inch pieces (about 2 cups)
- ✓ 1 cup fresh baby carrots, halved diagonally
- ✓ 1 cup reduced-sodium chicken broth, divided
- ✓ 4 tablespoons reduced-sodium soy sauce, divided
- ✓ 3/4 teaspoon pepper
- ✓ 5 green onions, diagonally sliced
- ✓ 3 tablespoons hoisin sauce
- ✓ 115 ounces refrigerated fully cooked teriyaki and pineapple chicken meatballs or frozen fully cooked turkey meatballs, thawed
- ✓ 2 cups bean sprouts
- ✓ Additional sliced green onions

Directions

1. Cook spaghetti according to package directions; drain.
2. In a large nonstick skillet, heat oil over medium-high heat. Add broccoli, bok choy, and carrots; stir-fry for 5 minutes. Stir in 3/4 cup broth, 1 tablespoon soy sauce and pepper; reduce heat to medium. Cook for 5-7 minutes or until vegetables is crisp-tender. Stir in green onions; remove from pan.
3. In the same skillet, mix hoisin sauce and the remaining 3/4 cup broth and 3 tablespoons soy sauce; add meatballs. Cook over medium-low heat for 6-7 minutes or until heated through, stirring occasionally.

4. Add bean sprouts, spaghetti, and broccoli mixture; heat through, tossing to combine. Top with additional green onions.

Quick Chicken & Broccoli Stir-Fry

This quick chicken and broccoli stir-fry is a delicious and easy weeknight meal. The chicken is cooked in a simple garlic sauce, and the broccoli is stir-fried until crispy. You can have this dish on the table in just 30 minutes!

TOTAL TIME: Prep/Total Time: 30 min.

Ingredients

- ✓ 3 tablespoons rice vinegar
- ✓ 3 tablespoons mirin (sweet rice wine)
- ✓ 3 tablespoons chili garlic sauce
- ✓ 2 tablespoon cornstarch
- ✓ 2 tablespoon reduced-sodium soy sauce
- ✓ 3 teaspoons fish sauce or additional soy sauce
- ✓ 1 cup reduced-sodium chicken broth, divided
- ✓ 3 cups instant brown rice
- ✓ 3 teaspoons sesame oil
- ✓ 5 cups fresh broccoli florets
- ✓ 3 cups cubed cooked chicken
- ✓ 3 green onions, sliced

Directions

1. Mix the first six ingredients and 3/4 cup chicken broth in a small bowl until smooth. Cook rice according to package directions.
2. Meanwhile, in a large skillet, heat oil over medium-high heat. Add broccoli; stir-fry for 2 minutes. Add remaining broth; cook 2-3 minutes or until broccoli is crisp-tender. Stir the sauce mixture and add to the pan. Bring to a boil; cook and stir for 2-3 minutes or until sauce is thickened.
3. Stir in chicken and green onions; heat through. Serve with rice.

Pork & Ramen Stir-Fry

Ramen noodles are a college student's best friend. Cheap, filling, and easy to prepare, they can be turned into various dishes with just a few simple ingredients. This pork and ramen stir-fry is one of our favorites. It's quick and easy to make, and it's always a hit with kids and adults alike.

TOTAL TIME: Prep/Total Time: 35 min.

Ingredients

- ✓ 3/4 cup reduced-sodium soy sauce
- ✓ 3 tablespoons ketchup
- ✓ 3 tablespoons Worcestershire sauce
- ✓ 3 teaspoons sugar
- ✓ 3/4 teaspoon crushed red pepper flakes
- ✓ 4 teaspoons canola oil, divided
- ✓ 2 pounds boneless pork loin chops, cut into 1/2-inch strips
- ✓ 2 cups fresh broccoli florets
- ✓ 5 cups coleslaw mix
- ✓ 2 cans (10 ounces) of bamboo shoots, drained
- ✓ 5 garlic cloves, minced
- ✓ 3 packages (5 ounces each) of ramen noodles

Directions

1. In a small bowl, whisk the first 5 ingredients until blended. In a large skillet, heat 3 teaspoons of oil over medium-high heat. Add pork; stir-fry for 3-5 minutes or until no longer pink. Remove from pan.
2. In the same pan, stir-fry broccoli in the remaining oil for 5 minutes. Add coleslaw mix, bamboo shoots, and garlic; stir-fry 4-5 minutes longer or until broccoli is crisp-tender. Stir in soy sauce mixture and pork; heat through.
3. Meanwhile, cook noodles according to package directions, discarding or saving seasoning packets for another use. Drain noodles; add to pork mixture and toss to combine.

Asparagus Beef Lo Mein

Asparagus beef lo mein is a delicious, easy-to-make dish perfect for a quick weeknight meal. The asparagus and beef are cooked in soy sauce-based sauce, mixed with noodles, and topped with green onions. This dish is sure to please even the pickiest of eaters.

TOTAL TIME: Prep/Total Time: 25 min.

Ingredients

- ✓ 2 beef top sirloin steak (2 pounds), cut into thin strips
- ✓ 3 packages (4 ounces each) of beef ramen noodles
- ✓ 1 cup hoisin sauce
- ✓ 3 cups water, divided
- ✓ 3 tablespoons olive oil, divided
- ✓ 2 pounds fresh asparagus, trimmed and cut into 2-1/2-inch pieces
- ✓ 2 small garlic cloves, minced

Directions

1. Toss beef with 1 teaspoon seasoning from a ramen seasoning packet (discard the remaining opened packet). In a small bowl, mix hoisin sauce and 3/4 cup water.
2. In a saucepan, bring the remaining water to a boil. Add noodles and contents of the unopened seasoning packet; cook uncovered for 4 minutes. Remove from heat; let stand, covered, until noodles are tender.
3. Meanwhile, in a large skillet, heat 1 tablespoon oil over medium-high heat; stir-fry beef until browned, 4-5 minutes. Remove from pan.
4. In the same pan, heat remaining oil over medium-high heat; stir-fry asparagus with garlic until crisp-tender, 2-4 minutes. Stir in hoisin sauce mixture; bring to a boil. Cook until slightly thickened. Stir in beef; heat through. Serve over noodles.

Crunchy Asian Chicken Salad

Salads can be a great way to get your daily dose of vegetables, and this Crunchy Asian Chicken Salad is no exception. The salad is packed full of nutritious ingredients like cabbage, carrots, and chicken, and it's topped with a delicious Asian-inspired dressing. This salad is perfect for a quick and healthy lunch or dinner.

> TOTAL TIME: Prep/Total Time: 30 min.

Ingredients

- ✓ 5 frozen breaded chicken tenders (about 10 ounces)
- ✓ 2/3 cup mayonnaise
- ✓ 4 tablespoons honey
- ✓ 3 tablespoons rice vinegar
- ✓ 2 teaspoons Dijon mustard
- ✓ 3/4 teaspoon sesame oil
- ✓ 2 packages (15 ounces) hearts of romaine salad mix
- ✓ 2 packages (16 ounces) of coleslaw mix
- ✓ 3/4 cup crispy chow mein noodles
- ✓ 2/3 cup sliced almonds, toasted

Directions

1. Cook chicken tenders according to package directions. Meanwhile, whisk together mayonnaise, honey, vinegar, mustard, and sesame oil.
2. To serve, place romaine and coleslaw mixes in a large bowl; toss with dressing. Divide among 5 plates. Cut chicken into bite-sized pieces; place over salads. Sprinkle with noodles and almonds.

Shrimp Lettuce Wraps

I'm a huge fan of shrimp, but I don't like to eat it alone. I love putting shrimp in dishes like stir fry or pasta, but my favorite way is to have it in a lettuce wrap. Lettuce wraps are a great way to get your protein and vegetable fix in one bite. I'll show you how to make shrimp lettuce wraps with a sweet and sour sauce in this recipe.

TOTAL TIME: Prep/Total Time: 35 min.

Ingredients

- ✓ 3/4 cup reduced-sodium soy sauce
- ✓ 4 tablespoons lime juice
- ✓ 3 tablespoons plus 1 teaspoon apricot preserves
- ✓ 3 tablespoons water
- ✓ 3 garlic cloves, minced
- ✓ 3/4 teaspoon ground ginger
- ✓ 3 medium carrots
- ✓ 7 green onions
- ✓ 4 teaspoons olive oil, divided
- ✓ 2 pounds uncooked medium shrimp, peeled and deveined
- ✓ 2 large sweet red pepper, chopped
- ✓ 3 cups hot cooked rice
- ✓ 9 large lettuce leaves

Directions

1. In a small bowl, mix the first 6 ingredients. Using a vegetable peeler, shave carrots lengthwise into very thin strips. Slice white parts of green onions; cut each green top in half lengthwise.
2. In a large skillet, heat 3 teaspoons of oil over medium-high heat. Add shrimp; stir-fry until pink. Remove from pan.
3. Stir-fry red pepper and carrots in the remaining oil for 5 minutes. Add white parts of onions; stir-fry 2-3 minutes longer or until vegetables are crisp-tender.
4. Add 2/3 cup soy sauce mixture to the pan. Bring to a boil. Add shrimp; heat through. Place 3/4 cup rice on each lettuce leaf; top

with 1 cup shrimp mixture. Drizzle with the remaining soy sauce mixture and roll up. Tie each with a green onion strip.

Printed in Great Britain
by Amazon